Original title:
Chains of Connection

Copyright © 2025 Creative Arts Management OÜ
All rights reserved.

Author: Juliana Wentworth
ISBN HARDBACK: 978-1-80586-052-5
ISBN PAPERBACK: 978-1-80586-524-7

Stars Aligned

In a bar where oddballs meet,
A dog wore socks on four small feet.
A cat cheers with a tiny hat,
Why not dance? You're all so fat!

With twinkle lights that set the mood,
Penguins shuffle, looking crude.
Jellybeans fly through the air,
Who knew snacks had so much flair?

The Embrace of Harmony

A parrot sings a silly tune,
While frogs croak just to bring the gloom.
An otter shows some funky moves,
As others groove, the rhythm soothes.

Bananas play a keytar role,
Rocking with passion, heart, and soul.
Laughter echoes through the night,
We're all weird, but it feels so right!

Connected Footprints

A squirrel scurries, chasing tails,
While turtles ponder grander trails.
Footprints follow like a game,
Who's the fastest? Who's to blame?

A chicken struts with urban pride,
Sneakers on, it can't abide!
Frogs leap, and friendship forms,
In our chaos, joy transforms.

Collective Journeys

We all hopped on a silent bus,
Baked beans decided to cause a fuss.
With giggles bursting, laughs arise,
As jelly rolls escape and fly!

Collecting quirks like shiny rocks,
In mismatched shoes and funky socks.
Together we're a sight to see,
Just a bunch of oddity!

Heartstrings Entwined

In a world of tangled threads,
We laugh at all the knots we've spread.
Silly ties that bind us tight,
We trip and tumble, what a sight!

With every laugh, our bonds grow strong,
Together we dance, we can't go wrong.
In this circus of goofy plays,
Our heartstrings play in silly ways!

The Flow of Kinship

Like a river that can't stop its flow,
We splash around with a mighty glow.
Giggling ripples of friendly jest,
In this stream, we're at our best.

Throwing jokes like stones in the creek,
The laughter rises; we hardly speak.
With winks and grins, we craft our fate,
What a party in this flowing state!

Together We Rise

On a trampoline of joy we bounce,
With every jump, our laughter pounces.
From silly falls to soaring highs,
Together we reach for the skies!

In a pile of pillows, we collide,
Squeaky giggles that we can't hide.
Up we go, tumbling with cheer,
With every bounce, we bring good near!

Serenade of Solidarity

In the choir of quirky tunes we sing,
Every note makes our hearts take wing.
With off-key laughter, we create our song,
In this joyful mess, we all belong!

Harmonious jests, our voices twine,
In this melody, we're just fine.
Side by side, in jocular embrace,
We serenade life with a funny face!

The Ties of Memory

In the attic, dust will play,
Grandma's stories go astray.
Tangled thoughts, a silly dance,
Mistaken dates, oh what a chance!

Photos fade, but joys ignite,
Mismatched socks within our sight.
Each laugh is a knot that binds,
Forgetful moments, clever minds!

Conduits of Connection

My phone can't stop its endless ring,
A cat meme sent—a solemn thing.
We share our woes, our silly rants,
Life's chaos in laughter chants!

A skit of life, our jokes collide,
Zoom glitches are our joyful pride.
Skittles thrown through fiber lines,
Snack-fueled antics, oh, such signs!

The Ties that Remember

Remember when we lost the plot?
At dinner's end, a cake forgot.
Uncle Joe with icing on nose,
We laugh till tears of memory flows!

A game of charades in disguise,
Dad's wild dance, oh how he tries!
Each moment's a bookmark, don't erase,
In our silly, shared embrace!

Interlaced Journeys

Our travel tales, a twisted map,
Got lost on roads, took a nap.
With every turn, a laugh erupts,
Navigation gone, but joy corrupts!

With odd souvenirs, we return,
A spoon from Texas, oh how we yearn!
Memories woven like thread and yarn,
In our scrapbook world, never a barn!

The Fabric of Friendship

In the tapestry of laughs so loud,
We stitch our stories, oh so proud.
With thread of quirks and bits of cheer,
We weave a bond that's crystal clear.

Through silly pranks and jelly spills,
We share our dreams and countless thrills.
A patchwork quilt of memories bright,
Our friendship shines, a joyful sight.

Bridges of Belonging

Across the gaps where gaffes may lie,
We build our bridges, oh my oh my!
With each goofy step and every jest,
We find our place and feel our best.

From wobbly walks to daring feats,
Together we feast on tasty treats.
With laughter echoing through the air,
We forge a bond beyond compare.

Hand in Hand

We're hand in hand, a quirky pair,
With high-fives flying everywhere.
In silly hats and mismatched socks,
We dance like clowns around the blocks.

Our strolls are filled with whimsical fun,
Chasing rainbows, never done.
With every giggle and playful tease,
We create a world that's sure to please.

The Knot that Ties

A knot so strong, but not quite neat,
It twists and turns on silly feet.
With double-backs and tangles tight,
We laugh together, what a sight!

In this wild loop of friendship's game,
We giggle loud and stake our claim.
With every tug and playful pull,
Our bond grows stronger, never dull.

Interlaced Journeys

Two lost socks in the dryer spin,
They share tales of where they've been.
Adventures with sneakers, oh what a sight,
Dancing with dust bunnies all through the night.

A cat and a mouse strike a deal,
To dance on the table, oh what a reel!
Together they laugh, a peculiar sight,
With bacon and cheese, they feast in delight.

The Symphony of Us

The piano's keys all start to play,
A catwalk for a rat in dismay.
Harmony found in an outlandish jam,
The trombone's slide makes the hiccup a slam.

Cookbooks scattered on the floor,
Spaghetti fights and a garlic war.
We dance with whimsy, that's what we do,
With each clumsy step, the laughter grew.

Embracing Common Ground

Birds in hats plotting a grand scheme,
To steal old bread and create a dream.
Down the lane, they hop with glee,
Chasing crumbs—such a sight to see!

At a picnic, ants host a feast,
While a careless dog plays the least.
Burgers fly while laughter abounds,
In this chaos, true joy resounds.

Shadows of Togetherness

Under the streetlight, the shadows meet,
A quirky dance, oh what a feat!
The tree's limbs reach, a playful embrace,
While the moon giggles in its own space.

Friends on the couch, popcorn flies up high,
As movies roll, they slip and sigh.
Each laugh a bond, a snicker, a cheer,
In the silly shadows, we're all near.

Bridges of Understanding

Two squirrels chat 'bout acorn stock,
While pigeons gossip near a clock.
A dog gives a knowing glance,
As cats begin their daring dance.

Beneath the noise, a friendship brews,
Connecting the weirdest of crews.
An iguana shares a secret with a bee,
As raccoons hold a tea party, full of glee.

Everyone finds a link in jest,
In their silly antics, they are blessed.
From garden gnomes to the wise old owl,
They all have stories that make us howl.

So let us laugh and share a chat,
With every critter, even the rat.
Despite our quirks, we all belong,
In this wacky world, we can't go wrong.

Ties Across Time

A dinosaur with a dapper tie,
Meets a rabbit in a bowler hat nearby.
The T-rex offers tips on fashion flair,
While the bunny just wants to win a hare's prayer.

Time machines and sneakers, let's go play,
Past and present, in a silly way.
Knights and astronauts share a joke,
While a time traveler tries not to choke.

The discussions range from pizza to pies,
Past lives revealed in each other's eyes.
The caveman thinks the future's a dream,
While the future man no longer screams.

So here's to moments that blend and twist,
Through giggles and gaffes, they coexist.
From ancient ruins to future cars,
Together they navigate, beneath the stars.

Unity in Disguise

A clown and a cat make quite the pair,
Each wearing shoes that lead to nowhere.
They juggle laughs and little slips,
As puddles form beneath their flips.

A chicken dances with a mouse,
Together they shock the quiet house.
Frogs in sunglasses croak a tune,
While bees waltz under the smiling moon.

In costumes bright and hats askew,
They create connections that feel brand new.
Magic happens when giggles blend,
In silly mixes, hearts will mend.

So strut your stuff in a wacky guise,
Together, we laugh 'til we're all surprised.
For in the laughter lies the truth,
That unity blooms, regardless of youth.

Beneath the Surface

A fish in a tux, looking quite dandy,
And a crab with a cane, oh so handy.
They gossip, they chatter, in bubbles they meet,
Sharing tales of their underwater fleet.

Above, a bird tweets about the scene,
While a turtle dreams of being a queen.
They float through stories with colorful flair,
In the depths, they are unaware of their care.

A seaweed dance party begins to unfold,
With the jellyfish spinning, oh so bold!
While clams clap together with a great array,
Creating a symphony, night and day.

As currents sway and tides align,
Different creatures twirl, a grand design.
Beneath the surface, laughter does dwell,
In their quirky world, all is well.

The Wings of Together

We flock like birds in silly flight,
Bumping beaks, what a sight!
With every flap, we tease and cheer,
Who knew a dive could cause a jeer?

Together we loop, a colorful crew,
Dodging the clouds, what else can we do?
With giggles loud, we chase the sun,
In this wacky race, we're all just one!

Interwoven Dreams

In tangled beds of dreams we lie,
Snoring symphonies fill the sky.
The cat joins in, a soloist proud,
As we wake up soaring, then sit on a cloud.

With mismatched socks and wild hair,
We juggle our plans without a care.
What's a little chaos between pals?
Laughter's the magic that ties all the gals!

The Balance of Belonging

We dance like penguins on a thin line,
Slipping and sliding, but feeling fine.
With flappy arms, we find our way,
Balancing laughter on a sunny day.

A pogo stick here, a yo-yo there,
Each twist a giggle, each bounce a dare.
Life's a circus, with us as the jest,
In this jumbled fun, we're at our best!

Harmony in Our Differences

Oh, what a mix, like fruit in a stew,
With quirks that sparkle, each flavor is true.
From silly jokes to a quirky dance,
We delight in our oddities at every chance.

With polka dots and stripes, we blend,
Creating a rainbow, let the fun never end!
In our goofy ways, we sing loud and clear,
Together in laughter, with love and cheer!

Bonded Threads

In the closet, socks collide,
Tangled up, they take a ride.
One goes missing, oh what a plight,
That stubborn left, just loves to fight.

These threads of fate, they pull and tug,
A dancing dance, a fabric rug.
Each twist a laugh, each turn a cheer,
Together we weave, just don't disappear!

Unseen Ties

Invisible strings hold us tight,
Like two magnets in the night.
Though you may trip, I'll hold you fast,
Unless you spill my drink—then you're outcast!

With secret winks and silent nods,
We navigate through life's odd rods.
Friendship's glue, it makes no sound,
But when I yell, you're always around!

The Fabric of Togetherness

We stitch and sew with laughter loud,
Dressed in quirks, we stand so proud.
One wears stripes, the other spots,
Fashion faux pas? Nah, we've got chops!

In this quilt of joy, we patch and play,
Crooked seams make the best display.
With every snip, a joke we share,
The fabric's fun, it's beyond compare!

Echoes of Affinity

In cafes, our laughs intertwine,
Your coffee's cold, but my tea's divine.
We share our stories, both silly and wise,
While the waiter rolls his eyes and sighs.

Each echo bounces, a playful sound,
In this goofy world, we're tightly bound.
With every quip, we gently tease,
Together we jolt, like a mild breeze!

Echoes of Connection

Two friends went out to eat,
Their laughter filled the street.
They shared a plate of fries,
Spilled ketchup from their eyes.

A phone call at the dead of night,
One says, "You've lost your light!"
The other laughs and cheers,
"Is that your way to say cheers?"

In every silly story told,
Through secret jokes, their bonds unfold.
Like echoes that won't quit,
They find joy in every bit.

The Power of Together

Two socks danced in the mix,
One got stuck in laundry's tricks.
"We're the perfect pair!" they'd shout,
Until one got lost, then pouted out.

A bird and a cat played mock fight,
One swoops down, the other took flight.
Together they make quite a scene,
Who knew, cats could be so keen?

They brew up laughter, joy, and fun,
Chasing shadows, just to run.
In their antics, they discover,
Friendship's power like no other.

Constellations of Affection

Two stars winked across the night,
"Shall we dance with all our might?"
They twirled in cosmic space,
Bumping into every place.

A comet joined with much delight,
"Let's crash a party, join the flight!"
They beamed with glowing glee,
Creating chaos, wild and free.

With silly selfies, they all posed,
In twinkling joy, each one enclosed.
Their friendship shone, a galaxy,
Brighter than all the stars we see.

Sacred Interlacing

Two noodles in a pot they'll twine,
One says, "Hey, do you drink wine?"
The other laughs and takes a sip,
"Let's toast to this saucy trip!"

A pair of mittens, snug and nice,
"Why can't we bond over rice?"
They knit their dreams with silly threads,
While dancing on the rooftop beds.

In laughter's light, they will embrace,
Life's quirks turn into warm grace.
Their woven stories twirl with flair,
Knitted bonds beyond compare.

Circle of Trust

In a room full of friends, some whispering lies,
One claims he's a chef, but his noodles just cry.
We share silly secrets, our laughter does swell,
Trust is a circle, where all tales can dwell.

With a wink and a nod, we spin wild old stories,
Like the time Joe danced, in all of his glories.
We roll on the floor, with a chuckle or two,
In this circle of trust, I'm just like you too.

The secrets we hold, are a comic relief,
Like the time Rita wore shoes made of beef!
In our bond, the nonsense is truly the best,
Together, we laugh till there's pain in our chest.

Unity in Diversity

A parrot that squawks like a cat at the moon,
And the cat replies with a sweet, silly tune.
Together they dance in a lively parade,
In this mix of oddities, friendships are made.

From the squirrel in shades, to the dog with a hat,
We live in a jungle, where giggles are at.
Each voice is a note in this quirky old song,
In the theater of life, where we all belong.

So here's to the moments we cheer and we tease,
Like the time Fred slipped, with a big slice of cheese!
In our eclectic mix, all laughter is grand,
Together we flourish, a wild, funny band!

Shared Echoes

Echoes of laughter bounce off the walls,
Every silly moment we share truly calls.
Like the time Bill juggled while bouncing on one,
We howl at the memory, oh what silly fun!

In a giggling chorus, our voices entwine,
Every joke, every pun, it's a treasure divine.
With a wink and a glance, we're united in jest,
Through echoes of giggles, our hearts feel the best.

From a mishap with glue, to a mishap with pie,
Our shared little quirks, like birds soaring high.
In this silly symphony, we'll dance and we'll cheer,
Together we echo, with laughter sincere.

Ties of Time

Time slips like butter on a sunny warm day,
With our quirks and our jokes, we just laugh and play.
A history written in giggles and grace,
Each moment we cherish, each silly face.

From the depths of our hearts, memories emerge,
Like the cake that we baked with a secret surges.
Each birthday a riot, a cake for the ages,
With frosting and sprinkles, like laughter on stages.

The ties that we forge, they grow stronger each year,
With absurd little moments that bring us all cheer.
In the tapestry woven with kindness and fun,
We cherish our ties, like the warmth of the sun.

Symbiotic Souls

You stole my fries, I'll share my pie,
Together we laugh, as the ketchup flies.
We borrow each other's socks each night,
In this quirky bond, everything feels right.

In a yoga class, you fell on my toes,
Together we giggle at the gym's weird flows.
You pop my bubble when I'm feeling shy,
Yet your jokes make me laugh until I cry.

We swap odd memes, like fine art,
Each GIF a masterpiece, a work of heart.
From coffee spills to advice misplaced,
In this madcap dance, we've found our place.

So here's to us, in a whirl and whirl,
Two silly souls, dancing in a twirl.
Our laughter echoes, a joyful ring,
In this crazy friendship, life's a fling.

Harmonious Links

You sing off-key, I start to sway,
Our random duets make the best of day.
I borrow your quirks, you wear my hats,
This joyful ensemble, how it all chats!

In the morning rush with a dash and zoom,
We spill our coffee, then share the gloom.
But laughter bubbles, brightens the mess,
We find the fun in this hectic stress.

You call me out when I dance like a fool,
Yet join in the chaos, breaking all rules.
With silly selfies, our weirdest pose,
In the gallery of goof, our friendship grows.

With you, life's a sitcom, each moment a treat,
From wacky adventures to snacks we eat.
So here's to our chorus, the sync we bring,
In this ludicrous harmony, let's laugh and sing!

Roots Intertwined

In a garden of friends, our roots intermingle,
We dig out the dirt, yet somehow still tingle.
With flower pots tipped, we dance in the breeze,
This botanical mess brings us to our knees.

You plant silly jokes, I sow all the puns,
Together we shine like two dazzling suns.
When I trip over daisies, you hold my hand,
In this tangled maze, we perfectly stand.

As weeds pop up between giggles and grins,
We dig up the laughter where true joy begins.
From wildflower crowns to the mess we create,
In our garden of chaos, we celebrate fate.

So here's to the roots that keep us entwined,
With laughter like rain, and good vibes combined.
Together we flourish, through thick and through thin,
In this garden of ours, let the fun begin!

The Network of Us

You send me cat memes, I reply with glee,
In this digital world, we're wild and free.
With tags and retweets, we brighten the feed,
Our virtual bond plants the silliest seed.

In a game of charades, you're quite the champ,
I try to act like a rather large lamp.
Yet we burst into laughter, can't hold it in,
Our network of joy, where the antics begin.

You once sent a postcard, but forgot the stamp,
Still, my heart got the delivery, a joyful lamp.
As messages bounce, our friendship grows wide,
In this playful exchange, we always collide.

So here's a toast to the laughter we share,
With phones in our hands, we're quite the pair.
In this web of delight, with smiles we fuss,
For in our little network, it's always a plus!

Tangle of Emotions

In a box of tangled wires,
I search for my lost keys,
A dance of mismatched feelings,
Like cats on a hot breeze.

Laughter echoes through the room,
As socks unite in streams,
Each hiding one odd partner,
Like lovers lost in dreams.

Balloons float to the ceiling,
Chasing each other in flight,
While ants march in a line,
Just trying to find some light.

Tickled by the silly mess,
We grin like fools in glee,
For in this tangled chaos,
Life's laugh is plain to see.

Threads of Unity

Like spaghetti on a plate,
Twisted and so fun,
Life pulls us all together,
Underneath the sun.

The coffee cup's relationship,
With the doughnut at its side,
A match made in happiness,
With sprinkles as their guide.

Yarn balls roll around the floor,
Tugging at the cat's whim,
Each purr a tiny thread,
Where joy is not so dim.

As we gather 'round the fire,
With marshmallows to toast,
These threads of glee unite us,
And that's what I love most.

The Ties That Hold

A shoelace tangled in a knot,
A saga of sheer wit,
We giggle at its stubbornness,
As shoes start to submit.

These ties may stretch and pull,
Like rubber bands so spry,
Yet in their silly stretching,
They stick with a wild sigh.

Friendship's like a pizza slice,
Each piece with cheesy flair,
Even when it's half-baked,
We share the love we care.

So let's tie up our laughter,
With bow ties made of cheer,
For those adorable connections,
Are what keeps us all near.

Interlocked Paths

Two paths meet at a crosswalk,
Where squirrels play hopscotch,
They argue over breadcrumbs,
That's the grandest botch!

With umbrellas gone rogue,
Dancing in the rain,
They spin like little beings,
Doing the should-have-wain.

The puddles splash like laughter,
They jump with squishy paste,
And shoes lose all their senses,
In this wet-footed haste.

Through all the funny twists,
We find our joy to glean,
For every step we wander,
Paints a bright laughter scene.

Where Shadows Meet Light

In the corner, shadows play,
They dance and twirl the night away.
A lightbulb flickers with a grin,
Saying, 'Let the chaos begin!'

With mismatched socks and quirks galore,
We stomp our feet and holler for more.
Like jellybeans in a puppy's paws,
Together we're silly without a pause.

The hallway echoes with our cheer,
We tube slide down without a fear.
Like bumblebees buzzing out of tune,
We fill the air with a silly swoon.

So here's to the goofy, the odd, and fun,
In this wacky dance, we're never done.
When shadows meet light, laughter ignites,
A carnival of glee in our sights!

The Tapestry of Us

Threads of laughter, vibrant and bright,
Stitching cozy moments, day and night.
We weave our stories, like a quilt,
In this fabric of life, joy is built.

With mismatched patterns, we celebrate,
Our tangled yarns can never negate.
Like cats on a yarn ball, we roll and spin,
Ties get tangled, but that's where we win.

We pull on the strings that keep us tied,
In joyous knots, we all take pride.
With jigsaw pieces that don't fit right,
Together we shine, a beautiful sight.

So let's keep weaving this quirky design,
In the tapestry of us, everything's fine.
Threading through laughter, tears, and trust,
Our patchwork of life is a must!

Ties That Bind

Like spaghetti loops on a dinner plate,
We twist and twirl, we say 'Aren't we great?'
In the grand banquet of highs and lows,
Our silly moments are the best that grows.

A rubber band flies, it's all in good fun,
Better duck quick before it's all done.
With mismatched cheers and goofy grins,
A raucous symphony of silly sins.

Like puppies bundled in a playful heap,
We build forts from pillows when we can't sleep.
The ties that bind us are made of jest,
With laughter as our armor, we silly quest.

So here's to the gaffes and goofy blunders,
With belly laughs that leave us in wonders.
In the crazy chaos where joys collide,
These funny moments, oh how they abide!

Whispers of Belonging

In the whispers of clumsy delight,
We spun tales under the moonlight.
With inside jokes that no one knows,
An orchestra of giggles in a row.

Like rubber chickens flying about,
Our playful hearts are never in doubt.
The hiccups of friendship bring us near,
With belly laughs spilling over the cheer.

We juggle our antics, not one can resist,
Moments we share, they top the list.
Like puppies chasing their own tails round,
In this silly circle, love is found.

So let's dance to the rhythm of play,
Where jokes and laughter hold the sway.
Whispers of belonging, a chorus of fun,
In this wacky world, we all are one!

Stories of Togetherness

In the park, we play and run,
Sharing laughs, oh what fun!
You lost your shoe, I found a hat,
Now we look like a silly cat.

At the cafe, we sip our tea,
You spill on me, I spill on thee!
Our clothes now sport a color spree,
Fashion tips from you to me.

On the couch, we binge and snack,
Cereal flies, watch it hack!
Popcorn battles, oh so grand,
You lose the fight, I rule the land.

Together we face the ups and downs,
With mismatched socks and silly frowns.
In every story, we find delight,
A goofy pair, oh what a sight!

By Our Side

You bought the milk, but spilled the soy,
In the mess, you feel the joy.
I'm here to help, just don't you fret,
We'll clean it up, no need to sweat.

In the kitchen, we burn the toast,
But laugh so hard, we feel like ghosts.
You dance around with a frying pan,
I'll be your biggest fan, yes, I can!

Umbrella upside down, we stroll in rain,
Parking lot wants us to jump the train!
Together we find the silliest ways,
To brighten up the dreariest days.

Side by side in this crazy race,
We'll trip over shoe laces, just embrace.
In this wacky world, we shine anew,
A duo that's wild, just me and you!

Reverberations of Love

You sing off-key while I hum along,
We create a tune that's all wrong.
Neighbors clap and beg for more,
Our concerts leave them at their door!

With every hop, our voices clash,
The dog barks loud, oh what a bash!
You twirl around, forgetting the steps,
But we can't help it, we're two happy reps.

In the park, we chase the ducks,
They quack in sync, oh, what luck!
We imitate their goofy quack,
And roll on the grass, no turning back.

Together we share this silly dance,
Life's a song, let's take a chance.
With goofy grins, we spread the cheer,
Reverberating love, that's our sphere!

Unseen Tethers

You took my fries, but that's okay,
Your sneaky moves make my day!
In the game of sharing snacks,
Our bonds get tighter, no need for hacks.

At the beach, you build a mound,
The waves crash down, but we're still around.
With sand in our hair and shells in hand,
We giggle and splash, oh isn't it grand?

You say I'm odd, I call you weird,
Yet in this friendship, we've both steered.
Our quirks create this joyful jam,
Together forever, maybe? I am!

In every moment, near or far,
We're linked together, that's who we are.
With laughter and love, we'll never sever,
These unseen threads connect us clever!

Embracing the Ties

We're stuck together, like peanut and jelly,
Two oddball socks, yet never too smelly.
You always crack jokes, I roll my eyes,
But without your quirks, I'd surely despise.

In the world of laughter, we dance like fools,
You trip on your shoelace, but hey, who needs rules?
With silly faces, we brighten the day,
Connected by laughter, come what may.

You steal my fries, I swipe your last bite,
We laugh so hard, it feels so right.
Through thick and thin, we stay on track,
Like a mismatched pair, we'll never look back.

As we wobble through life, hand in hand,
Making memories, just like we planned.
It's crazy and fun, this bond we weave,
In this hilarious mess, we truly believe.

Echoes of Unity

We echo our laughter, bouncing around,
Like two rubber balls that roll on the ground.
Your jokes hit the mark, mine flop like a fish,
But we laugh it off, as if it's our wish.

In silly debates, who's right, who's wrong?
We argue for hours, but still sing our song.
Your snorts and my giggles create quite a scene,
In the comedy club, we reign as the queen.

Like a hilarious skit, we're quite the team,
In the theatre of life, we're living the dream.
Tripping on punchlines and slipping on cheese,
Through humor and chaos, we do it with ease.

With each funny story that we combine,
We build our own world, perfectly aligned.
Here's to the moments, the laughs we will share,
In this echo of joy, there's love everywhere.

Web of Kindred Spirits

In this tangled web, we spin and we play,
Like cats in a box, we pounce every day.
Your quirks are my treats, my goof is your prize,
We're two clowns in a circus, just look in our eyes.

Knock-knock jokes echo, we both feign a laugh,
Like two awkward penguins trying to dance half.
In this chaos of chuckles, we find our own beat,
With oddball rhythms, we're never discreet.

Through highs and lows, we dance like a breeze,
With silly routines that bring us to knees.
Your dance moves are awkward, mine can't compete,
Yet we rock the floor with our happy defeat.

Together we sparkle, a wacky parade,
In the museum of laughs, our bond won't fade.
A tapestry woven, with giggles and cheer,
In this web of wonders, you're always near.

Inextricable Threads

We're stitched together, like a quirky quilt,
In the fabric of fun, all laughter is built.
Your puns are so bad, they make my head spin,
But in this ensemble, we always win.

With mismatched colors, we stand tall and proud,
Making a ruckus, drawing in a crowd.
Your wild tales echo while I make a face,
In this zany journey, we've found our place.

Our lives intertwine like spaghetti and sauce,
Every twist and turn, we just laugh and toss.
In the comedy of errors, we find our stride,
Two clumsy bumblers, but love can't hide.

As we tackle this world, hand in hand we go,
Through laughter and joy, we steal the show.
In our tapestry woven, with threads oh so bright,
Together forever, we're a glorious sight.

Clusters of Companionship

In a world of quirky friends,
We laugh until we bend.
With pranks and playful tease,
We find our joy with ease.

From socks that disappear,
To inside jokes my dear,
Together we make a scene,
Like a wacky, wild routine.

With lunchbox swaps and schemes,
We share our silliest dreams.
A tribe that's oh so loud,
We're a ruckus-loving crowd.

In mischief and delight,
We soar to silly heights.
With laughter in the air,
Who needs a dull affair?

Invisible Bonds

Like ghosts in funny hats,
We dance with our mishaps.
Invisible threads we weave,
In pranks you won't believe.

Oh, the stories that we share,
Of silly things laid bare.
With every laugh and glance,
We bloom in goofy dance.

Sometimes we trip and fall,
Our balance? Not at all!
Yet through the bumps we roam,
In this madness, we find home.

So here's to our weird spree,
A wild crew, full of glee.
These bonds will never break,
Even when we're wide awake!

Reservoirs of Gratitude

With grateful hearts we sing,
For all the joy you bring.
From snacks to jokes we share,
Each moment filled with care.

In coffee spills and treats,
We find our silly feats.
A treasure chest of smiles,
That stretches for miles and miles.

You brought the quirks, it's clear,
Like laughter in a beer.
With every silly chat,
Our friendship grows like that!

So let's toast with our mugs,
To all the friendly hugs.
In this vast, joyful sea,
I'm so glad you're with me!

Alliance of Hearts

In this league of laughter loud,
We're a most peculiar crowd.
With puns and jokes galore,
We're never, ever a bore!

Through every silly prank,
In friendship, we give thanks.
With hearts as light as air,
We float beyond all care.

From movie nights to snacks,
We plan our little hacks.
Together we'll succeed,
In laughter, we are freed!

So join the joyful ride,
With you, I'll always side.
In this wonderful affair,
We thrive beyond compare!

Threads of Hope

In a web of laughter, we all get stuck,
Trying to find joy with every bit of luck.
A grandma's poodle jogs by with a shoe,
We chase after dreams, like kids after goo.

The coffee's brewing, but where's the cream?
Oh wait, it's inside my wildest dream!
We trip over socks, our ties in a knot,
Yet through silly moments, we find what we sought.

A raccoon steals snacks, while we dance and sing,
Life's little surprises make the heart take wing.
We tumble through giggles, as we crash and bump,
In the chaos of connections, we take a fun jump.

So let's paint the sky with our wacky hues,
With every small folly, we banish the blues.
In this circus of life, under bright, twinkling lights,
We revel in mishaps, our laughter ignites.

The Gravity of Bonds

Oh, the weight of friendship, what a funny thing,
We pull each other close, then yank on a string.
Like magnets on roller skates, we wobble and sway,
In this goofy game, we just want to play.

My buddy's a hoot, with his lasagna hat,
He trips on his laces—oh, look at that!
We twirl through the mess, arms flailed in delight,
Each tumble a story, each laugh a highlight.

When the pie hits the floor, we all burst with glee,
We're the silly salad, you just wait and see.
As we gather our thoughts, with fries on the side,
In this bouncy buffet, let's feast with pride!

We're tied together, like spaghetti and sauce,
In the dance of our lives, we're the whimsical gloss.
So let's munch and crunch while the music plays on,
In this gravity of bonds, we'll always belong.

Fusion of Paths

We stumbled together on a bicycle spree,
Two riders, one seat, oh what a sight to see!
With legs all a-tangle and giggles so loud,
We conquer our fears like a daring young crowd.

On this kooky adventure, we climb up the trees,
With squirrels as our guides, we share our cheese!
We leap over puddles, land splashes with flair,
In this fusion of paths, we soar through the air.

Our jumbled directions lead to paths unforeseen,
Like kittens on skateboards, we roll so serene.
We'll turn every stumble into dance and parade,
Through the absurd journey, sweet memories are made.

So here's to the misfits, the silly, the free,
In the loop of our lives, let's have jubilee!
With jokes and confetti, let's laugh 'til we fall,
In the fusion of paths, we'll cherish it all.

Weaving Hearts

In a room full of socks, my heart takes flight,
Matching patterns make me feel so light.
Dancing with laughter, we tumble and spin,
Each goofy move is where joy begins.

With spaghetti noodles all tangled and twirled,
We share our dreams, oh what a strange world!
Who knew that sauce could create such a bind,
Cooking with friends, we're a laugh riot combined.

On roller skates, we zoom without care,
With helmets snug, we float in the air.
Crashing like comets, oh what a surprise,
Spinning in circles, it's hard not to cry.

A jigsaw puzzle missing a piece, oh dear,
We search for the square while we sip on our beer.
Each sly remark and a wink in the fray,
In this goofy chaos, we find our way.

Links of Destiny

In a café where spoons are often misplaced,
We bond over coffee and the odd cupcake waste.
Each frothy sip holds secrets untold,
In this sweet moment, our laughter unfolds.

The cat that stole fries from my plate last week,
Brought us together, a bond unique.
Chasing a feline through puddles and grime,
We giggled and stumbled, oh what a time!

With sock puppets dancing and making a scene,
We create silly stories with zest in between.
Who knew our hearts would connect with such flair,
Entertained by our art, we made quite the pair.

As we juggle with lemons, hoping for luck,
Life throws us curves but we just laugh it up.
In the comedy of life, we all take a part,
Tangled in joy, we strengthen the heart.

Entangled Lives

A game of charades, we act out our dreams,
With crazy gestures and ridiculous themes.
Guessing ambiguous hints that we share,
Our laughter escapes, swirling in the air.

Dodgeballs and chaos at the park today,
Dodging and diving while kids jump and play.
One wild throw sends us all to the ground,
In this furry pile, joy knows no bound.

With mismatched gloves and hats on our heads,
We roast marshmallows over sizzling reds.
Sticky and sweet, we embrace the delight,
In this silly mess, everything feels right.

And in every mishap, we find something grand,
Fumbling together, it's truly unplanned.
In the dance of connection, our hearts align,
Entangled in laughter, oh love's sweet design.

The Web We Spin

We weave a tale of blunders so bright,
Tangled like yarn in the shadiest light.
With every stitch, our laughter unwinds,
In this whimsical world, joy always reminds.

In attempts to bake, oh what a delight,
Mixing flour and sugar till we take flight.
Pies on our faces, the kitchen a mess,
Here's to our struggles—it's pure happiness!

With random dance-offs in grocery aisles,
We flip, we twirl, and we flash goofy smiles.
Carts filled with laughter, we cheerfully scoot,
Each strange little moment, a flavorful fruit.

The web spans wide, stitched with bright glee,
Tales of mishaps, oh just wait and see!
From pranks to puns, in this life that we spin,
The threads of our lives, let the laughter begin!

Links of Understanding

We chat and laugh, a silly call,
Our puns and jokes, they never fall.
In playful jests, we find our way,
Each typo turned to comedy's play.

A wink, a smile, a wink in text,
Who knew our words would be so vexed?
With memes and gifs, we share our days,
In oddball ways, we laugh and blaze.

Complicated thoughts distilled to cheer,
A pondering mind, but no one's near.
Through giggles lost in the tangled web,
Connections found in each tiny ebb.

A world of fun within our reach,
Absurdity's lessons, we both teach.
So let's embrace this quirky ride,
In humor's grip, we both abide.

Ties that Bind

In mismatched socks, our colors clash,
Yet somehow, we still make a splash.
With laughter echoing 'round the room,
We lighten up even the darkest gloom.

A friend in need with coffee stains,
Our blunders shared, our silly gains.
In perfect chaos, we find our groove,
Like dancers lost, we still can move.

When life gets tough, we joke on through,
With silly hats and bright balloons too.
Each playful jab, a friendly tease,
In giggly tones, we find our ease.

Through trials tossed like a wobbly kite,
Together, we shine, a comical sight.
For bonds are formed in laughter's embrace,
With silly faces, we find our place.

Weaving Togetherness

With yarns of laughter, we knit and purl,
Our conversations spin, twirl, and swirl.
Each silly tale a thread in the woof,
Stitching together our goofiest proof.

A tapestry bright with colors bold,
In every joke, a secret told.
With crafty tags and punny prods,
We dance through life, giving it nods.

In this fabric of folly, we weave our fate,
Stitching the quirks that we imitate.
Through every snicker and chuckle's chime,
We tie our lives, a rhythm and rhyme.

In humorous patterns, our bonds align,
Woven delight, a vibrant design.
From laughter's loom, we craft a cheer,
In threads of joy, we hold each dear.

The Tapestry of Us

In vibrant hues, our stories play,
Each thread a giggle, brightening the day.
With clumsy footsteps, we take a leap,
A dance of mischief—oh, look! I tripped!

Upon this fabric where tales collide,
With playful mischief as our guide.
Each blunder made with hearts aglow,
In a whimsical patchwork, we grow.

Laughter mingles with moments grand,
Through curious tales, hand in hand.
In this mosaic of clumsy words,
We find the joy, like flocks of birds.

So let's revel in this crazy ride,
With laughter bright, we'll not divide.
For in this tapestry, our hearts will trust,
It's the laughter and fun, that is a must!

Together in Silence

In a room full of chatter, we sit side by side,
Eyes glued to our phones, yet we're full of pride.
Sharing memes about cats, it's a riot, you see,
Laughter erupts, though it's just you and me.

Silent agreements, a nod and a grin,
Unspoken thoughts, where do we begin?
Your joke about pickles gets me every time,
In our quiet corner, we're perfectly in rhyme.

Unplanned adventures, like running in rain,
Jumping in puddles, what's life without pain?
Pretending we're graceful, we trip on our feet,
Two goofballs together, oh life is so sweet.

In this bubble of quiet, joy's laughter runs deep,
With you by my side, who needs beauty sleep?
The world may be loud, but we've made our own space,
In stillness, we thrive, an unending embrace.

Threads of Affinity

A kitchen disaster, oh what a delight,
Mixing cake batter, it flies like a kite.
You spill on your shirt, I'm covered in flour,
Together we giggle with sugar and power.

Our mismatched socks tell stories untold,
In a whirlwind of colors, we're vivid and bold.
You stole my last fry, but I'll let it slide,
Because sharing a laugh is the sweetest of pride.

Tangled up in our plans, the cat takes a leap,
Creating new chaos, breaking our sleep.
Yet laughter resounds, in the mess we embrace,
Like threads in a tapestry, we find our own place.

In a world that spins fast, we wander in slow,
Building our dreams from the seeds that we sow.
With every mishap, our bond grows more bright,
We may be a circus, but it feels just right.

Bonds Beneath the Surface

In a crowded bar, we play rock-paper-scissors,
A strategy game, who knew you were a wizard?
Your laughter is like bubbles in fizzy champagne,
We're two goofy pirates, steering through the rain.

Witty comebacks that fly in the air,
You call me a fish, but not out of despair.
The dance of our voices, a comedic duet,
We've got our own rhythm, with laughs to beget.

As we text our secrets, emojis galore,
Your wink makes me giggle, who could ask for more?
Underneath the surface, a bond that's alive,
Like quirky sea critters, we happily dive.

In the tapestry of life, we're the wildest of threads,
Sailing on laughter, where joy gently spreads.
So let's keep it silly, and never lose track,
With bonds like these, there's no turning back.

Interwoven Hearts

In a park for the weirdos, we share our odd tales,
Feeding the ducks while wearing bright veils.
Your stories of aliens crack me up wide,
With laughter that echoes, I'm full of pride.

Intertwined on our swings, like kids in a dream,
Swing higher and higher, we giggle and scream.
Those squeaks of the metal, our soundtrack of glee,
Who knew friendship could feel so carefree?

You stole the last cookie, but I won't hold a grudge,
With crumbs on your face, you leap and you trudge.
Through humor and warmth, our hearts find a beat,
In the quirkiness found, we craft our retreat.

Life's a wild ride, through valleys and hills,
With laughter to guide us, and silly thrills.
So here we remain, in this jubilant spree,
With interwoven hearts, forever carefree.

The Pulse of Togetherness

In a room full of giggles, we sway,
Collecting moments, come what may.
Our laughs like butterflies take flight,
Tickling the air, oh what a sight!

Jellybeans rolling on the floor,
A dance-off starts, who could ask for more?
We spin and trip, it's quite a show,
Our antics adorned with a silly glow.

With snacks in hand, we form a pact,
Riding our bikes, and that's a fact!
Falling into puddles, splashes loud,
Together we're silly, a goofy crowd.

So here we are, a quirky team,
Living life like it's a dream.
From pranks to puns, we keep it bright,
In the pulse of fun, we take our flight.

Fragments of Us

Pieces of laughter crash and collide,
Like mismatched socks, we take it in stride.
We stumble and bumble, that's our style,
Crafting memories that make us smile.

A puzzle unfit, with corners askew,
Yet every odd piece fits perfectly too.
Banana peels and tickle fights,
Fumbling over jokes, sparking delights.

Our quirks form a tapestry bright,
Like mismatched shoes, a quirky sight.
In this jigsaw where nonsense reigns,
Together we dance, embracing the gains.

Reflections of us in a fun dance,
Falling in puddles, we take a chance.
With laughter as glue, we build our way,
Fragments of joy that choose to stay.

Threads of Love

In a web of giggles, we spin our tales,
Like spaghetti monsters with wobbly sails.
We toss around puns like confetti in air,
Creating a chaos that we all share.

Each thread a story, awkward yet bold,
With socks on our hands, the fun's uncontrolled.
We yarn our way through every odd day,
Knitting memories in the silliest way.

From puddle jumping to dance-offs galore,
We've woven our laughs, can't ask for more.
Through tickles and snacks, we build our space,
Threads of bright joy, we gleefully embrace.

So here's to the laughter, the light we weave,
In this colorful quilt, we bravely believe.
Tangled yet smooth, our tapestry's spun,
With threads of delight, we're never outdone.

Weaving Dreams

In a land of zany, where giggles bloom,
We weave our dreams in a colorful room.
With bubblegum laughter and thoughts that soar,
We tie two shoelaces, what a chore!

Our dreams like marshmallows fluffy and sweet,
Jumping in puddles with happy feet.
We throw on capes and become superstars,
Chasing our fantasies beneath the stars.

From slipping on ice to misreading maps,
Our journey is full of oops and mishaps.
But every slide, every twist, every whirl,
Makes the fabric of life a colorful swirl.

So let's toast to laughter and dreams woven tight,
With bubbles and jokes, we'll dance through the night.
In the tapestry of friendship, we find our way,
In weaving wild dreams, let's always play!

Symphony of Support

In the concert hall, we all play,
With squeaky chairs that sway and sway.
A tuba's honk, a trumpet's flair,
Together we laugh, no room for despair.

When one goes flat, we all go sharp,
A little off-key, but still a harp.
With mismatched socks and silly ties,
Music of friendship always flies.

Clapping hands in perfect time,
A chorus of giggles, oh so prime.
The rhythm of life, a jolly jest,
With everyone's quirks, we love them best.

So here's to the band, our motley crew,
In perfect discord, we always grew.
With each note played and each pun dropped,
In our joyful symphony, we never stop.

The Echoing Embrace

In a big ol' room full of squishy chairs,
We're all sharing stories in our silly wares.
A whoopee cushion, a squeaky toy,
Echoes of laughter, our ultimate joy.

When someone trips, we all just fall,
A domino stack, we can't stand tall.
Giggles erupt like popcorn in air,
An embrace of humor beyond compare.

With high-fives given, and hugs gone wild,
We flip the script, like a goofy child.
Dance like no one's watching, so free, so bright,
Together we shimmer, in pure delight.

So here's to the giggles, so rich and rare,
In our echoing vibes, life's wonderful affair.
With each silly moment, our fun's embraced,
In this silly romance, none goes to waste.

We Share the Weight

If I'm feeling heavy, feel free to lift,
In a game of burdens, the best kind of gift.
We stack our troubles like a pancake stack,
But add some syrup, and we'll bring it back.

With giggles galore, we can lighten the load,
Even a rock can become a toad.
When life gets tough, we'll bring in the cheer,
A punchline in hand, we'll persevere.

Through thick and thin, we laugh and we sigh,
In this merry mix, we're all flying high.
Like juggling pies as we run down the street,
Together, we dance, on our awkward feet.

So here's to the moments, we share and collide,
In this circus of life, you're right by my side.
With every shared giggle, our weight feels light,
In this joyful journey, everything's bright.

Celebration of Togetherness

Let's throw confetti, a colorful blast,
In our quirky clutches, we're holding fast.
With mismatched hats, and balloons in the air,
The party's ignited, with laughter to spare.

When one does a dance like a chicken in flight,
We join in together, what a beautiful sight!
From piñata mishaps to cake on the face,
In this carnival chaos, we find our place.

With each silly toast, we raise up our cups,
To the laugh that erupts when the humor erupts.
A banquet of giggles, a feast of delight,
In our celebration, everything's right.

So here's to our crew, dancing under the moon,
In this wild celebration, we'll sing our tune.
With smiles so big, and hearts like a feather,
We dance through this life, forever together.

Minds Aligned

We gather for a coffee, each face a quirky sight,
Jokes fly like birds, oh what a hilarious flight!
We share our wildest dreams, everyone's in the race,
Who knew sharing a latte would turn this place into a space?

A shared love for the bizarre, oh what a silly spree,
We gab about the squirrels, driving cars—can't you see?
With every laugh we share, we stitch our stories tight,
Tangled in laughter, we embrace the light!

From baking fails to pet tales, we're a comedic crew,
Laugh lines like rivers, endlessly flowing through.
In this madcap circle, we become a raucous song,
A merry band of misfits where all of us belong!

So raise your glass of soda, let's toast to pure delight,
With minds forever linked, we dance into the night!

The Spiral of Kinship

We spin upon this dance floor, what a dizzy little crew,
Twisting and twirling, it feels like déjà vu!
Every step is laughter, a joyous, clumsy game,
With each clumsy pirouette, we uplift our shared name!

In mismatched shoes and ties, we stumble on the beat,
Our rhythm may be scattered, but this fun can't be beat!
The laughter echoes loudly as we whirl from side to side,
A merry-go-round of friendship, on this raucous ride!

We trip over our own feet, but that's just part of the charm,
Like jellybeans in a bowl, we can't resist the calm.
With every laugh we share, we spiral into glee,
Dizzy with connection, just let it be, let it be!

So here's to all our missteps, each giggle and our cheer,
We're like a dizzy maze, with nothing left to fear!

Confluence of Souls

We meet at the buffet, what a colorful display,
With plates piled high, oh what a feast today!
From silly soup debates to dessert that steals the show,
A flavorful concoction of friends that we all know!

In every bite, a laugh, what a savory blend,
We're a potpourri of stories, where every fork can mend!
Each side dish has a tale, from grandma's secret pie,
We merge our lives like flavors, let our spirits fly!

As we dig into each story, voices swirl and twine,
Like pasta on a fork, our lives start to align.
From the spicy to the sweet, our hearts begin to toast,
In this banquet of stories, it's friendship we love most!

So let's feast on this feast, in laughter and delight,
For in this gathering of souls, everything feels right!

Beneath the Same Sky

We lie on grassy hills, gazing up with a grin,
Counting stars together, letting wild tales begin.
"Look! That one's a puppy!" someone exclaims with glee,

Another sees a taco, "I must be hungry, you see!"

We share our wild imagination, each star a brand new tale,

A comet's just a pizza delivery gone astray in the gale!
From aliens at the barbecue to bumpkin sightings galore,
Under this canopy, we create myths to explore!

In this cosmic comedy, we laugh 'til we cry,
What a zany venue, just stars and us on high!
With dreams woven in starlight, we're joyful and bold,
Connected beneath the heavens, our laughter won't grow old!

So let's lie here forever, with giggles in the air,
Underneath this same sky, life is sweetness, we declare!

The Dance of Togetherness

In a room full of laughter, we spin and twirl,
Tripping over feet, watch the chaos unfurl.
With mismatched socks and shoes a bright hue,
We flail like a fish, but we're not through!

Holding hands like a train, we wobble around,
Laughter erupts at the slips we have found.
A two-step disaster, it's fun, what a sight,
Together we bumble, from day into night!

Each leap and each twirl tells a tale of our glee,
The rhythm is silly, oh, just let it be!
Knees knocking, we giggle, let nothing be wrong,
We're all in this together; come dance along!

So join us, dear friend, for this grand, funny ride,
In every misstep, our joy will abide.
Through the laughter and folly, we'll find we belong,
In the dance of togetherness, we ever stay strong!

Spheres of Understanding

We gather like planets, so varied and bright,
In our own little orbits, we take our flight.
With quirky ideas that bounce like a ball,
In this cosmic game, there's space for us all!

Each thought is a comet, zooming high in the sky,
They pass with a flash, we laugh and we sigh.
From strange notions of life to our wildest of dreams,
These orbs of a thought form a laughter-filled stream!

In circles we go, with a fruitcake parade,
Discussions like planets, dancing unafraid.
We spiral together in our unique way,
In this galaxy of fun, forever we'll play!

So pop into our universe, join in the cheer,
Where misunderstandings just disappear.
In the spheres of our minds, the joy never ends,
Through laughter and banter, we're always good friends!

Reflections of Connection

In the mirror of life, we all strike a pose,
Grinning at goof-ups, that's how it goes.
With faces like clay, we shape and we mold,
In this funhouse of mischief, the stories unfold!

A wink and a nod, we watch and compare,
Hairstyles gone rogue, with flair and a dare.
Each giggle a ripple on this pond of delight,
Our reflections are silly, oh what a sight!

We bounce off each other like shadows in play,
Roaring with laughter at the games that we sway.
In this carnival of quirks, we all find our tune,
Playing hide-and-seek with a runaway balloon!

So catch a reflection of joy in each glance,
Together we bubble, in our silly dance.
Through laughter and fun, we all come alive,
In this crazy kaleidoscope, together we thrive!

The Unity of Differences

In a gathering of quirks, we stand side by side,
Like a buffet table, where flavors collide.
With pickles and ice cream, it's hard to believe,
In our whacky world, there's magic to weave!

Every oddball idea is a gem shining bright,
In this quirky assembly, we all share the light.
From hats worn askew to our mismatched delight,
Together we sparkle, day turns into night!

So raise your odd drinks, and give them a toast,
To the charm of our differences, we celebrate most.
With laughter and cheer, one and all we unite,
In this fun-loving tapestry, everything's right!

In this silly fusion of peace and of glee,
We embrace our oddities; it's wild and free.
So come one, come all, to this colorful spree,
Together we flourish, just you wait and see!